CABLES TO THE ACE

or

Familiar Liturgies of Misunderstanding

For Robert Lax

"La mise en question du monde dans lequel nous sommes
ne peut se faire que par la forme et non par une anecdote
vaguement sociale ou politique"

A. Robbe-Grillet.

By Thomas Merton

BREAD IN THE WILDERNESS

CABLES TO THE ACE

CLEMENT OF ALEXANDRIA

EMBLEMS OF A SEASON OF FURY

GANDHI ON NON-VIOLENCE

NEW SEEDS OF CONTEMPLATION

ORIGINAL CHILD BOMB

RAIDS ON THE UNSPEAKABLE

SELECTED POEMS

THE STRANGE ISLANDS

THE TOWER OF BABEL

THE WAY OF CHUANG TZU

THE WISDOM OF THE DESERT

EDITOR: BREAKTHROUGH TO PEACE

Published by
New Directions

CABLES TO THE ACE

or

Familiar Liturgies of Misunderstanding

THOMAS MERTON

A NEW DIRECTIONS BOOK

PROLOGUE

You, Reader, need no prologue. Do you think these
Horatian Odes are all about you? Far from the new
wine to need a bundle. You are no bundle. Go advertise
yourself.

Why not more pictures? Why not more rhythms, mel-
ody, etc.? All suitable questions to be answered some
other time. The realm of spirit is two doors down the
hall. There you can obtain more soul than you are ready
to cope with, Buster.

The poet has not announced these mosaics on purpose.
Furthermore he has changed his address and his poetics
are on vacation.

He is not roaring in the old tunnel.

Go shake hands with the comics if you demand a preface.
My attitudes are common and my ironies are no less
usual than the bright pages of your favorite magazine.
The soaps, the smells, the liquors, the insurance, the
third, dull, gin-soaked cheer: what more do you want,
Rabble?

Go write your own prologue.

I am the incarnation of everybody and the zones of
reassurance.

I am the obstetrician of good fortune. I live in the social
cages of joy.

It is morning, afternoon or evening. Begin.

I too have slept here in my stolen Cadillac.

I too have understudied the Paradise swan.

May 1967

CABLES TO THE ACE

Lament of Ortega. The crowd has revolted. Now there are bathrooms everywhere. Life is exempt from every restriction!

I

Edifying cables can be made musical if played and sung by full-armed societies doomed to an electric war. A heavy imperturbable beat. No indication where to stop. No messages to decode. Cables are never causes. Noises are never values. With the unending vroom vroom vroom of the guitars we will all learn a new kind of obstinacy, together with massive lessons of irony and refusal. We assist once again at the marriage of heaven and hell.

2

A seer interprets the ministry of the stars, the broken gear of a bird. He tests the quality of stone lights, ashen fruits of a fire's forgotten service. He registers their clarity with each new lurch into suspicion. He does not regret for he does not know. He plots the nativity of the pole star, but it neither sets nor rises. Snow melts on the surface of the young brown river, and there are two lids: the petals of sleep. The sayings of the saints are put away in air-conditioned archives.

3

Decoding the looks of opposites. Writing down their silences. Words replaced by moods. Actions punctuated by the hard fall of imperatives. More and more smoke. Since language has become a medium in which we are totally immersed, there is no longer any need to say anything. The saying says itself all around us. No one need attend. Listening is obsolete. So is silence. Each one travels alone in a small blue capsule of indignation. (Some of the better informed have declared war on language.)

4

Letters to a corridor: "Put the whole family out into the hall." (Plato) Now they are outside receiving those hard cosmic cables without interception.
Ideas, productions, answers: sand in the eye. He who has the most sand in his eye thinks he sees everything.
It is written: "To see the world in a grain of sand."
Science, Politics, Theology: sandstorms.
Does anybody sing? Some will try the following hymn.

5

Gem notes
Of the examiner
Or terminal declarations:

The Directors
Have engineered a surprise
You will not easily discover:

(Escape in a carload
Of irritated pets
Before the examination)

Come shyly to the main question
There is dishonor in these wires
You will first hesitate then repeat
Then sing louder
To the drivers
Of ironic mechanisms
As they map your political void

You will be approved
By parakeets and lights
For many original
Side-effects
Each nominal conceit
Will be shot down by an electric eye
Your poem is played back to you
From your own trump card

Until all titles are taken away
Events are finally obscure forever
You wake and wonder
Whose case history you composed
As your confessions are filed
In the dialect
Of bureaux and electrons.

6

*You taught me language and my profit on't
Is, I know how to curse. The red plague rid you
For learning me your language!*

(Caliban)

4

7

ORIGINAL SIN

(A MEMORIAL ANTHEM FOR FATHER'S DAY)

Weep, weep, little day
For the Father of the lame
Experts are looking
For his name

Weep, weep little day
For your Father's bone
All the expeditions
Dig him one.

He went on one leg
Or maybe four
Science (cautious)
Says "Two or more."

Weep weep little day
For his walking and talking
He walked on two syllables
Or maybe none

Weep little history
For the words he offended
One by one
Beating them grievously
With a shin bone.

8

Write a prayer to a computer? But first of all you have
to find out how It thinks. *Does It dig prayer?* More

important still, does It dig me, and father, mother, etc., etc.? How does one begin: "O Thou great unalarmed and humorless electric sense . . ."? Start out wrong and you give instant offense. You may find yourself shipped off to the camps in a freight car. Prayer is a virtue. But don't begin with the wrong number.

9

"I am doubted, therefore I am. Does this mean that if I insist on making everybody doubt me more, I will become more real? It is enough to doubt them back. By this mutual service we make one another complete. A metaphysic of universal suspicion!" (These words were once heard, uttered by a lonely, disembodied voice, seemingly in a cloud. No one was impressed by them and they were immediately forgotten.)

10

Warm sun. Perhaps these yellow wild-flowers have the minds of little girls. My worship is a blue sky and ten thousand crickets in the deep wet hay of the field. My vow is the silence under their song. I admire the woodpecker and the dove in simple mathematics of flight. Together we study practical norms. The plowed and planted field is red as a brick in the sun and says: *"Now my turn!"* Several of us begin to sing.

11

What do you teach me
Mama my cow?
(My delicate forefathers
Wink in their sleep)

6

"Seek advancement
Then as now
And never learn to weep!"

What do you want of me
Mama my wit
(While the water runs
And the world spins)
"All the successful
Ride in their Buicks
And grow double chins"

What do you seek of me
Mama my ocean
(While the fire sleeps
In well baked mud)
"Take your shotgun
And put it in the bank
For money is blood."

12

Another sunny birthday. I am tormented by poetry and
loss. The summer morning approaches with shy, tenta-
tive mandibles. There are perhaps better solutions than
to be delicately eaten by an entirely favorable day. But
the day is bright with love and with riches for the un-
concerned. A black butterfly dances on the blond light
of hot cement. My loneliness is nourished by the smell
of freshly cut grass, and the distant complaint of a
freight train. Nine even strokes of the bell fall like a
slowly counted fortune into the far end of my mind
while I walk out at the other end of awareness into a
very new hot morning in which all the symbols have to

be moved. Here is another smiling Jewish New Year and the myths are about to be changed. We will start up brand new religious engines in the multiple temples. Tonight the dark will come alive with fireworks and age will have scored another minor festival.

13

(THE PLANET OVER EASTERN PARKWAY)

In the region of daffodils
And accurate fears
We seek the layout
The scene of claims

We expect 8 A.M.
With cries of racers
"Here is the entrance
To the start"

And the smart pistol
Glints in the eyes
Of an eternal chief
He sees executives
Begin to run
Over fresh cut graves
The whole civic order
Of salads
Blest and green
By order of the town.

Then the machine
With sterling efforts
Keeps in trim

In tune with oil
Though it needs essential grooves
Say the keepers

And you are always turning it off
Says the owner.

So now it is over
The day of executions
Malfeasances are over and done
In all the books of law

And the cart wheel planet
Goes down in the silos of earth
Whose parkways vanish in the steam
Of ocean feeling
Or the houses of oil-men

Go home go home
And get your picture taken
In a bronze western
An ocean of free admissions
To the houses of night
To the sandy electric stars
And the remaining adventures
Of profiteers.

14

Some may say that the electric world
Is a suspicious village
Or better a jungle where all the howls
Are banal.

NO! The electric jungle is a village
Where howling is not suspicious:
Without it we would be afraid
That fear was usual.

15

They improve their imitable wire
To discover where speech
Is trying to go.

They guess it goes
To the sign of the ear
Talking of portable affairs

Splitting into little mills
Of magnets and seconds
The everlasting carbon vine
A smooth investigation

Paying off into all the vessels and portholes
Of known lawgivers
Who learn the time of the carrier
And the arriver

Relaxed war-gods
Unlock the newest ministry of doors
With capital letters

The seeing line discovers dread
Tracks silvery doom's
Inventive car

Through all electric walks
And expert lights
It commands dawn riders

Lenses discover blue flame
In the mouths
Of fatal children

Parades and takeovers
Follow the parable
Wherever normal.

16

Let choirs of educated men compose
Their shaken elements and present academies of
     electronic renown
With better languages. Knowing health
And marital status first of all they must provide
Automatic spelling devices or moneymaking
Conundrums to program
The next ice-age from end-to-end
In mournful proverbs

Let such choirs intone
More deep insulted shades
That mime the arts of diction
Four-footed metaphors must then parade
Firm resolution or superb command
Of the wrong innuendo

You may indeed be given free of charge
An uninhibited guess
Three pensive norms

But no norm is necessary
For scholars and ages.

Then in the last resort suggestions
Will be wishful and make up erratic formulas
To obtain the best vowel or most
Expensive consonant

If you agree in the end
That in most cases
The best word of all is "ONLY"

17

How it can be done
Without delay

We are seeking ambitious men
Who have captured the sheer fascination
Of Marcus Aurelius
Havelock Ellis and the Marquis de Sade.

We can afford
Top pliable males
Who have always been boys at heart
Drag-racing through darkest Esquire.
Ready to become style leaders
And medium shapes
Hard as nails
Mean as the half-stewed owls we detest

Taking double-breasted advice
On barbells and heart-attacks
With friendliness and sex
At instant command

Able to afford
New areas of mind
With habit frequency and jags
And breathless weekends
Of instant mind-power
For the unusual partner
Or the executive bald on top
But ready to switch
And meet the challenge
Of the next instant
Always looking
Six inches taller.

18

He speaks cautiously to the Tea phone when it invites.
He considers the velleities of sixty. He has biblical man-
ners up his sleeve, this Old Master. He will often eat
fresh flowers. He is without imperative urges. He worries in his sleep; worries about the code. When he wakes
he will have forgotten all his lines. Can such a one have
presence of mind? His sons will not be as he is for he is
never strange.

19

Studies of man's friendly competitor the rat have shown
That pencils of control can find
Ways out for the withdrawn

Methods are right here says Dr. A for one
(Hiding the sockets in a troubled
Man whose friendly competitor the rat
Is pressing buttons and having fun.)

Man's friendly rat the competitor can prove
Wearing a cap on the vulnerable skull
That the absence of any motive is itself a mover

(*He suddenly looked around*
He spoke out loud
He met and talked with normal
Minds and research

Found fifty persons all with wires in the pleasure center
They were being moved by rats.)

There was more bliss in the tingling doorbell
Of long dead reward
Another man had periodic spells
And even ecstasies
Could he help it if the rat
Kept pressing?
It was a joy
For epileptics to wire
Home to their dead fathers
A long-distance call
Via your own brain
It is like a good feeling but where will it end?

Split second doses of motivation
Keep you in stitches
The potential is enormous
And the pointless smile
Will freeze without delay
An entire parlor

After warning the rat
He worked his own button to death

Back went the fires of ecstasy
And blew the rat sky-high.

Will my rat ever recover?
Will he call again
Ringing the septal region
That earthly
Paradise in the head
Two millimeters away
From my sinus infection?

Political man must learn
To work the pleasure button
And cut off the controlling rat
Science is very near but the morbid
Animal might always win

"It works like a bomb he declared after"

For a split second the competitor beams
All the lighted winners
Suddenly shine together
Like a big city
And at the end of the line stands Santa Claus
With his "Ho-ho" friendly to man

Maybe it could last
If the defender's smile
Were fixed in place by a
Clever surgeon

It can be made to last on rats
Studies of man's friendly competitor the rat

Have shown.

To sons: not to be numb.

Be a lone dog
Little brother
And paddle
Down the crowded street
With sleet in your eye
Killing all the Fathers
With your cigarette.
In the lobbies
And elevators
Be a cloud of hailstones
A visible episode
Or a migrant flame
Feeding on nothing
An anti-prophet
A dry homeless tree
With a knife in your side
And many skinny years to die in
As a life member of the unemployed.

20b

To daughters: to study history.

Finn, Finn
Tribal and double
Wide awake rocks
The fatal craft
Cutlash Finn
To kill time
Before and aft—
Er he sinks his fin
Again in his
Own Wake.

Next! The Guards hitch up their belts and look around
for another one who has been lazy, ineffective. Another
one who has shirked duty (and ALL have shirked it).
Political malingerers evading their obligation to believe
in the GREAT MEANING and to work at this belief,
purifying it of personal idiosyncrasy, doubt, guilty reser-
vations, etc. (Some still cultivate attachments and loyal-
ties which are opposed to the GREAT MEANING.)
The Guards hitch up their belts and look around. It is
their duty to teach. They will not hold back or neglect
their work. All their disciplines will *speak!*

22

Twelve smoky gates flame with mass-demonstrations.
Power of Caliban. Mitres of blood and salt. Buildings
    as well-run machines with eyes and teeth (Bosch).
Love the inevitable! Hate alone is perfectly secure in its
    reasons.
Over the door of Hell is written: *"Therefore!"*

23

Rock shot chasms
Promise unplanned flight
Little or no support
Choice is led
Out of bounds
Over the edge:
A slight change
The way is vague
Directions not precise
One method might be
To grow wings in time

And overplay
There is no right
Or wrong way
Here is only theory
The cultivation of air
In all the finals
Results will be awarded
Cheerful names.

24

Bernstein! Can you still hear me? Are you conscious?
(Leaning over ears. Talking to all the cities.)

25

Elastic programs to draft nonspecialist energy and rotate
funds to speedup intake of output: an imperial takeoff!

26

Corporate posture: variables of fat. Move payloads from
room to room. The vulgar replies of the ill tempered
clavicle: imported drinks on a mandatory and immov-
able base. But smiling. Management in the lump is fitted
out for meetings. Roomy handshakes amid displays and
breakthroughs. "We can definitely secure government
aid for Santa Claus!" This way we can be our own
news as well as read it.

27

"Hats off," cried the midget. "Hats off to the human
condition!"

The wounded football hero
Is nominated to share
In the human condition
Which he smilingly calls
"Straight fact."

His monumental force
With lovable drives and loads
Now gains at last
A prizewinner's compassion.
The media will name him
Like the name of some big building
Others will call him "Sandy" and
The "Polo King" or just "Mister Charlie"
He will be the leader in handouts
And a high school Socrates
Just as much at home
With the kids on the road
As with the capsule in the stars
Smiling out of all the groggy news prints
In the front seat or in the rumpus room.

And everybody knows
Why they gave him a name
Like some big building
Nominated to share
In the human condition:

He is coming
To investigate.

29

Since you and I became engines
Undamaged by blast or heat
Meeting the long curves
With royal welcome and style
We have wandered wherever we went
And filmed the latest effect
Of cartridge rivals

Since we began to be glad
With economy and popular acclaim
We knew sheer action pleasure
Was the nicest thing about owning
Our obsolete
Round-trip invention
Since we gained speed
And turned bright-green in space
We went backstage and met
The legend of air-cooled impulse
In time to regret it

Since when we have become umpires.

30

Morning
The chatter of meats
In jail and color bar
Nine o'clock boil
Traffic and coffee
Funerals in the shade of power
Crowds
Move in cotton mist

And chloroform
Slowly consumes
The energy of motors
An electric goat's head
Turns and smiles
Turns and smiles
Ten stories high
Emerald and gold
But a clergyman goes by
With a placard
"You can still win."
Night sanctuaries
Imaginary refuge
Full of flowers
Dimly lighted bottles
The solemn twittering of news
Names Omens Tunnels
Time to walk
Trustfully
Beside the killer
The image in the magic
Dark tree
The iron voice in the next apartment
Cries NOW
And you flush the toilet.

31

That's the girl in the middle, the one who will show you
her four nude feet any time. Yes, it's swingy tonight in
moongarden ten. But don't blush or run. What is blame
to a scrappy little sweetie like her? Tell 'em hon'. Come
and scud along down with "Bonnie Braes" and beam a
kiss to old vampire Tsars up yonder. You'll swell till

you go down again and it's time to swing out with the goodest little sonnysmokers and talk hips to this affluent Monster. Or cool it with a lucky crumb. Someday you'll see it, though they claim that's not possible: Beach tempo fighting the guitars for the dawn cigarette in the gates of an enemy factory. That's certain. It's all in the full knowledge of Uncle Sled. Trained lions can tell there's another heavy-duty load on the way, yes, loaded with double fun. And Swedes, too, Swedes from the local cooperation!

32

Don't go unhappy
To the ultraviolet home

You will be met at the next detour
By a squad car
Full of heroes

Now the psycho-
Electric jump
Into spasm:
A ticking spark

Feels great
Kills the snakes
And the odor of heresy

Now meet and kiss
The civic spirit
Marry virtue
In the nearest available alley

Handout
Bluegreen leaflets
Double meanings
A liberal beginning

While the Commander
And all the heroes
Stand around
In good condition.

33

Sartre said Francis Ponge had a moss-complex. Francis
Ponge should have replied that Sartre had a root-com-
plex. But they were not calling each other names. Nor
will I call them names either. We all have the same
anxieties—but we do not use the same words. Sartre
thinks words are saliva. Sartre must have a slobber-
complex. Actually of course all the words are gendarmes
and they stand around us in good condition. But Ponge
delights in his anxiety of cities, seeing them as shells,
skulls, bones, hardened secretions, rarely as pearls. Ang-
kor and Nimes turned out to be shells that were better
than oysters. And what of New York? "Let man," says
Ponge "trim down his words (or shells) to his own size
and do without a monument."

34

The sweetgum avenue leads to a college of charm
Where nubile swimmers learn to value
The exercise of pendulums
And join a long line
Of unreliable dials

For a nominal fee one can confide in a cryphone
With sobs of champagne
Or return from sudden sport to address
The monogag
The telefake
The base undertones of the confessional speaker
Advising trainees
Through cloistered earphones.

Oh the blue electric palaces of polar night
Where the radiograms of hymnody
Get lost in the fan!

The followers of St. Radegund
Rise like one man
On escalators to the new creation
The safe home base of the thunder
The stores of mildest snow
And the liturgical top floor where the future of art
Is revealed to knowers
In corduroy cathedrals.

35

Je vous lis les sonnets d'un capitaine aveugle. Il a les yeux
pleins de beaujolais. Il chante le partage des communions
electriques. L'or et l'argent tintent au sommet du Building *in extremis.*

C'est l'heure des chars fondus dans le noir de la cité.
Dans les caves, les voix sourdes des taureaux mal rêvés!
l'océan monte dans les couloirs de l'oeil jusqu'à la lumière des matins: et ils sont là, tous les deux: le Soleil
et le Franc-Tireur.

Poseidon embourbé mange les drapeaux sur la scène des guerres. Il contemple les ruines qu'il aime. Il considère les lois du naufrage. Il médite le commerce des algues. Il entend le son des perles.

Le jour douteux s'embrase à mesure des exhalations. C'est suprême! Le petit feu des argots consume les entretiens. C'est l'escalier orné de questions futiles qui conduit au Magistrat installé sur les étages les plus informes de la pensée. Message féminin! Tu nous attends dans le miroir obscur. Tu nous fais adorer les marchandises des astres, les dynamismes babyloniens.

Descendus de la scène des anges, les mots propres se cherchent parmi les hirondelles.

Platon est là avec les girls. Il les écoute. Il les encourage. Il reste inconnu. L'art devient propice aux cirques d'hiver. Dans la vallée des pleurs, le championnat du smile.

Vers l'abîme: les yeux de fer, les lampes ailées, les fuites autour du pôle. Le soleil brun des antipodes est armé de flèches. Il poursuit l'oiseau candide en fil-de-fer plumé d'orages. C'est l'instant du nerf qui éclate. Le bloc sourd de la sensation. Enfer intime du verbe neutre. L'oiseau se pose enfin sur le dôme des foudres.

Beauté hirsute de l'arsenal réveillé! Le petit barbu, le consul de cuivre, mâche les fumées insondables. Il contemple les arcs-boutants, les ponts navrés, les boucs en folie. Ce sont des enfants du cycle: des marins volages.

Il a vu le feu de ses narines, la flamme du socle. Amateur! Il revêt son manteau bordé de sang. Il marche à travers les cibles. Gavé de peines il respire la montée du sel. Il entre dans le traffic des noces. Il y est englouti tout plein de chansons païennes.

La mer Rouge des Pharaons, où le spectacle disparaît dans un chômage de vues, disparition des bien pensants! Les hiéroglyphes essaiment dans les temples du poulpe. Le sacerdoce masqué se promène encore au fond des mers à la recherche d'un Moïse perdu.

Les Mamans. Elles vivent sur les toits. Elles forment les petits oiseaux. Elles ont compris la sagesse de l'oeuf. Elles te proposent la patience et le délire. Elles te sourient au moment de ton choix. Ne choisis pas le neutre. Le front vendu ne te regarde pas O fleurs! signes du plaisir!

La tortue est fière de ses joyaux. Elle étend ses paumes pour les montrer à la pluie.

Fantoche traqué dans la givre voyeuse! Tu nous a embaumés comme des vers à soie. Va-t-on chercher ton Apocalypse dans les souterrains peu connus?

Je m'assieds dans mon champ vert comme un diamant tranquille. J'aborde le domaine bleu de l'air nu. Lumière et somme: la musique est une joie inventée par le silence. Pâquerettes. Toute une géographie de petites filles inconnues dans l'herbe. Charme des monstres enfantins. J'écoute le bourdon rouge des étés, le messager des temps sonores.

Nuage et testament. Je me tais à l'ombre des larmes. Je plains le muscle inutile qui crie: "Moi."

La frontière. Un peu plus loin. Elle est vert-clair. Le sommet. Rien! Les jeunes filles silencieuses entrent dans l'ombre par la porte des élues.

36

Eve moves: golden Mother of baroque lights. She visits a natural supermarket of naked fruits. She wings her perfumes. Le poil humide de ses aisselles. T. S. Eliot is vexed and cannot look.

37

The perfect act is empty. Who can see it? He who forgets form. Out of the formed, the unformed, the empty act proceeds with its own form. Perfect form is momentary. Its perfection vanishes at once. Perfection and emptiness work together for they are the same: the coincidence of momentary form and eternal nothingness. Form: the flash of nothingness. Forget form, and it suddenly appears, ringed and reverberating with its own light, which is nothing. Well, then: stop seeking. Let it all happen. Let it come and go. What? Everything: i.e., nothing.

38

Follow the ways of no man, not even your own. The way that is most yours is no way. For where are you? Unborn! Your way therefore is unborn. Yet you travel. You do not become unborn by stopping a journey you have begun: and you cannot be nowhere by issuing a decree: "I am now nowhere!"

39

"No man can see God except he be blind, or know him except through ignorance, nor understand him except through folly" (Eckhart).

40

Good Morning! Address more inspections to the corporate tunnels. Yours truly.

41

Approved prospect of chairs with visitors to the hero. Temperature is just comfortable for a variety of skins. It is with our skins here that we see each other all around and feel together. We are not overheated, we smell good and we remain smooth. No skin needs to be absolutely private for all are quiet, clean, and cool. The right fragrance is so right it is not noticed. The cool of the whole area is like that of a quiet car and presences. No one is really ailing and no one is quite that tired. See the pictures however for someone elsewhere who is really tired. Hear the sound of the music for someone who is relaxed (with an undercurrent of annoyance). She is glad to be sitting down with her limbs as if her long legs were really hers and really bare. This year the women all worry about their skirts. But she is well arranged. Whether they walk or sit they manage to be well arranged. In any case all is springlike with the scent of very present young women which with all our skin we recognize. Nothing is really private yet each remains alone and each pretends to read a magazine. But each one still smuggles a secret personal question across the frontiers of everybody: the skin of the body and the

presence of the scent and the general arrangement.
Nothing is out of place or disapproved. One by one each
skin will visit the hero.

42

Listen with a tremor to the aero-captain
Who cries: "Try harder!"

And the undaunted martial amputee
Swings in the sky his mountainous limb
For an artificial twelve mile gain
Today, today he is sworn in
As player and caller
Victor and frenzy
By the wild thousands
In their after dinner swoon.

Listen with a tremor to the aero-captain
Who cries: "Do it harder and go further!"

Then will the clever mechanic of haloes
Footprint over again the gameleg ball

By way of exception
The basketface hero
Snores an aero-dream
And hears his own captain exclaim
"I nominate your lost member
This year's leader in profit and loss
In saving common sense
By reason of high flight
Superlative reach
And uncommonly
Spacious habit."

"Strive more imposingly but only at the edges"
Cries the aero-voice!

43

Let us cool your bitter sweet charm with incense and verse
Praising our own comparison with a rich pigment
A new glaze of ours to make you the piquant
Awareness of yourself as enriched with our orchid temper
Mated to our lubricant to melt away
Stubborn little worries known as lines
To restore with magic lanolin our flawless picture of
   YOU
Yes you, our own pity-making sweet charade of oils
We love you with ease on immediate contact
Melting all the tell-tales and sorries
Refuting secret age with our petals of discipline
Our tender departures and unstuck pageantries
And always every day brand new reasons
For not despairing of your own
Fragrant velours.

We will make you into an air-conditioned wishing well
Afloat or abroad we will decorate your
Favorite place with monograms of daring souls
And instant specialists of flavor charm and grace
To win you baroque lawns
And crystal suitings
For your (day off) *Samedi du plaisir*.

44

Future of transgression. It is in the homes of Caliban.
A splendid confusion of cries. Politics of the inflexible
moon-calf. A martial display of bulldozers. Dull energies

in the dust of collapsing walls. Loose minds love the
public muscles of death.

45

(PRAYER TO SAINT ANATOLE)

Anatole Anatole the long jets
String their hungry harps
Across the storm
When everybody cries
In the chemical flame

Anatole Anatole the giant
Fivestar Generals
Riot and War
Bring us in fast cars
To the fire's Republic

To sing their loud
Steel tunes
Those burning blues
For body and soul
Saint Anatole

Anatole Anatole
The fairy bombers
The fatal recorders
The electric lyres.

46

Milton's fiends—Republican, bituminous—begin their
scenarios in the dark stink of burning gasoline. Batman,
the hero of hell, plots the ruin of New York. He has this
advantage: he cannot be consumed by fire.

47

Now the unruly knowing
Weather vane may falter
And be a bad actor
On the encrusted stilt
Of a newly serene
Mind-reading danger

Now the observer tells a lie
Or fixes the marred eye
Of unreflected sin
Inflames the conscious
Bleeding lights
Of so many full freeways
Out of a very ready city

Oh he severely conns
All interested railways
In the heavenly darkness!

He announces the blood-red minute
To go down to get in the earth
To be tightly locked in
As waif and vain hope
In the paddy cellar of fools

Grabbing the snug automatic
Restoratives digests
High fidelity tools
With other vitamin scores and residues

And obsolete information
Like: "No callers
No riders!"

48

Children of large nervous furs
Will grow more pale this morning
In king populations
Where today drug leaders
Will promote an ever increasing traffic
Of irritant colors
Signs of this evident group
Are said to be almost local

Today a small general open space
Was found lodged in the immediate shadow
Of the heavenly pole. It was occupied
Early in the week by Russian force teams
Their symbols are thought
To be unexplained

In New Delhi a fatal sport parade
Involving long mauves and delicate slanders
Was apprehended and constrained at three P.M.
By witnesses with evening gestures
In a menacing place where ten were prohibited
Many others were found missing in colossal purples
And numerous raided halls

All important Washington drolls
Continue today the burning of forbidden customs
Printed joys are rapidly un-deciphered
As from the final page remain
No more than the perfumes
And military shadows
President says the affair must now warn
All the star-secret homespuns and undecided face-makers

33

Today's top announcement is a frozen society
Publicizing a new sherbet of matrimonial midways
And free family lore all over the front pages
You will meet frank old middle age
With bold acquaintance soon forgotten
In the time sequence
Of an unbearable cycle
So drop the unacquainted
It is marked down
As an illegible name
Too soon for identification.

Atoms are bound to go said Nobel
Prize-waging Physic swinger
In an unpacked science stadium announcement
   Wednesday
He was clapped into recognition
When he was discovered
Suddenly full of crowds.

Martian Doctors recommend a low-cost global enema
To divert the hot civet wave now tending
To swamp nine thousand acres of Mozambique
Our Gemini spores and other space observers note
Small inflammations in the Northern Lights
And remedies beat all aspirin to these same Lights
For further confusion
Consult your ordinary delay
Or wait for the clergy.

A clear-cut daily exercise was taxed out of existence
By Communist thought-control today in a warring
House of votes where Senator Tolling Bell
Announced a bright green apology to wives

Deprived by the abolition
But much more fun he decreed
Would soon come of it as fortunately
Only few were present.

You can now win three-cornered advantages in the
    well known
Moon-section of Chicago which is filled since Thursday
With inventions of unprecedented laughter.

49

A lone train alarms the summer silence with a contralto
trident. The old man has won seven nights in formalde-
hyde. He has become a fixture. Go collect the lame tear-
drops of the Dog Star! Who will tell this fine gentleman
his fortunes are wintering? Well, he sings for it!

50

Give me a cunning dollar that tells me no lie
Better informed
Truth-telling twenties
And fifties that understand

I want to carry
Cracking new money
That knows and loves me
And is my intimate all-looking doctor
Old costly whiteheaded
Family friend
I want my money
To know me like whiskey
I want it to forgive
Past present and future

Make me numb
And advertise
My buzzing feedbacking
Business-making mind

O give me a cunning dollar
That tells the right time
It will make me president and sport
And tell me all the secrets
Of the telephone.

I want to know the new combinations
In my pocket I need to possess
Plato's Mother I want
What knows all the scores
And I want my money
To write me business letters
Early every day.

51

Look! The Engineer! He thinks he has caught something! He wrestles with it in mid-air!

52

Each ant has his appointed task
One to study strategy
And one to teach it
One to cool the frigidaire
And one to heat it.

Each ant has his appointed round
In the technical circuit
All the way to high
One to make it and the other to break it.

And each has his appointed vector
In the mathematical takeoff
In the space-supported dance
The comedy of orders.

And each must know the number of his key
With a key in his eye and an eye for numbers
A number of appointments
A truly legal score:
And each must find his logical apartment.

Each ant has his appointed strategy to heat
To fuse and to fire at the enemy
And cool it down again to ninety-nine
In the right order—
But sometimes with the wrong apparatus.

53

I think poetry must
I think it must
Stay open all night
In beautiful cellars

54

Amid the cries of gang walls and surprises the echoes
come forward. They are nude. A brazen charm expands.
It invests the unguarded senses. Twin stars rise over the
library. Another day lives. It questions the waterworks,
it knows the fevers of Vegas.

55

Outcry. A circus on another planet. The hero does not
trust the evidence of verbs. What evidence? The proof

has very long shores. Hunger. Six o'clock! Stark orations in the terminal. Waiting. Will incense increase in the radiators? The banging old tempest in the rooms of Tenth Street. Leaden echo. The bare tree. The faithless vow. We make the best of bad beginnings and hope the end will do better. Come, Dark-Haired Dawn!

56

On the long road of winding steel
The river road
A messenger comes
With modest anxieties
To seek me in the underworld of waiters.

I sing quietly to the immediate heart
One more wild hope dies of affliction.

The blue girl fumbles with her books and bags. She goes and will never return. That is as it must be every day.

Crowned wells are forming at every table.

A journal of drugged foundations. Sad interludes of rubber weather. Drink Chablis and wait, while crabs crawl backwards into the dumbwaiters. Curtis is in the kitchen troubled with his enemies and all their mean sayings. In his own worried way. A call is issued for nine wreckers to make a long story short in the elevators.

One more wild hope
Dies of affliction

57

Formerly we knew
Years of peaceable system

In which were organized
Chemical wanderings in the paint works
For the civilized and upright
Who could safely view
The rape of Sabines
Secured by Andrew Carnegie
With hat in hand
He surely thinks
Of priceless Flemings

Wandering in secret
Among all his paintings
Uprooted industry follows
A Sabine fortune
Hat in hand
By his presbyterian sense of smell
All his mind
Lost to fortune
All his poems torn.

58

The pencil continues to grieve with long questions in
the same lounge full of sea walkers. All the mailmen
study my friendless state holding back the letters. Behind the curtains placid grooms are looking for scandal.
They won't stay long in this temple of spenders, this
house of grammar and of wine. Will the deceiver wait
longer? In the crowd of beautiful callers one more wild
hope dies of affliction.

59

Our infantry is combing the hideouts
For faults in the enemy's prose
As reported in the extras.

60

Oh, said the discontented check, you will indeed win like
it says in the papers, but first you have to pay.
The bridges burn their builders behind them.
    The colored weepers try their luck with strings.

61

I will get up and go to Marble country
Where deadly smokes grow out of moderate heat
And all the cowboys look for fortunate slogans
Among horses' asses.

62

"Abandon your body and soul into the abundance of
light sent from above and give no thought to enlighten-
ment or illusion. Only sit like a great void of fire.
Breathe quietly. Concern yourself with nothing. . . . Be
like a completely dead man . . . empty of your own will
and of your own ideas. Think of what you cannot think.
In other words, think Nothing." (Dōgen)

All very fine, but his wall is full of cracks. The winds
blow through in every direction. He claims his light is
out and secretly turns it on again to read novels. He
builds a big fire to keep beginners warm: give him
credit for his kindness.

63

Uncle Sam with a knife at his throat
Holds out one hand to shake he promises hell
And he smiles.

Inhabited by a bear
He has to shine he is so eager for joy
And the bear is so thirsty.

Any old animal is secure inside a patriotic bust
Jealous of fresh air the heartbreak world
Is keen on coffee alone and forgets pain.

Ready for night to fall for Ursa Major
To come to light again and extend
A giant claw
Saying "Good Luck mister you can go to hell."

Now with a fortune in weapons and a cowboy riding his
    mind
Uncle Constellation gallops headlong down the sky
To the pure gems of Texas oil and firebird lotteries
And napalm in the magazines and bandits
Come forward eager to be recognized in person
Carried away with implements
To break more bottles with a convivial star
With stallions in the lucky wind
Flaming away like saloons or gone
In the unlucky airborne cars.

64

Note to subversives: Uncle has two extreme right hands
and means business!

65

It was already raining. They discovered all the bags
were empty. They walked slowly toward the gray cars.
They now knew for sure they had lost the same day
twice: once in sand, and once in water.

66

Oh yes it is intelligence
That makes the bubble and weather of "Yes"
To which the self says "No."

Science when the air is right says "Yes"
And all the bubbles in the head repeat "Yes"
Even the corpuscles romp "Yes."

But lowdown
At the bottom of deep water
Deeper than Anna Livia Plurabelle
Or any other river
Some nameless rebel
A Mister Houdini or somebody with fingers
Slips the technical knots
Pops the bubbles in the head
Runs the vote backwards
And turns the bloody cooler
All the way
OFF.

67

This is how to
This is with imperatives
I mean models
If you act
Act HOW.

Do this
When you are missing
Your home address
HUSTLE!

Because ours is a culture of bare-
Faced literal commands:

Go, Buster, GO!

68

(THE PROSPECTS OF NOSTRADAMUS)

In a yoke of steel laughs
Deathloving Jacks
Fly jungle bugs
Their fire loves creeps
They rain down love
On jungle creeps.

Tomorrow the alarm
And Mamas shrilling in the halls
Will play to win
Deathloving Jacks come home
And Mamas win
With green and purple wigs
Their eyes are ringed in lavender
They play for love
When yoked in jungle fun
Their creeps fly home.

In sixty-nine
When leftist moles assay
Our chrome Ideal
And we resist with lucky numbers
And wrong connections
Pocohontas a jungle nun
Returns to win the prize
Outwitting Mamas

And Jacks burn creeps again
In home town fun
That's seventy-one.

In seventy-three
Right-handed Jacks
Skilled in steel techniques
Issue wry alarms
And jokes of fire
The all-star population
Opens in a demon movie
Where cities bubble and pop
I see the champs are creeps
And leftist moles
Play for connections
And play to win
Deathloving Jacks drop their hot cards on living winners
("Thinking of you")
I hear the green-wigged cities
And their jokes of glue.

Seventy-four
Hot yules
London laughs and folds
Capetown swept
Johannesburg is crisp and cold
Where all the creeps have crept
Rio, Caracas, Mexico
Borrow the winning movie for another go
A day of Jacks and cleaners
When love melts Fort Knox Gold

Seventy-six
The gas is getting low

Some cities are out of air
All-star Mamas
Need all the water for their bluegreen hair
A year of frantic moles and drunken doves
Of killer mice and insect winners
Jacks without ammo fight with knives and knucks
A mystic capsule drones
Answer to pop explosion
O fill the empty tank with dooms of love!

The Eighties open with a twotime Easter
Day of a monster clam
No decision and no sound
From the hermetic tomb
No raids or bulletins
Until a simple one-two device
Ignites the champion explosion
And the Giant Mongrel takes over
With a tee-hee combustion
Followed by mists and politicians
In family-sized capsules
Well-provided
Fly for Orion.

Eighty-nine
Day of the grunt
The incision
The killer rat
All the lavender wigs are gone
The last of Jacks and Mamas
Have electronic hospitals on moon.

Two-thousand
Year of the low tone

Berlin:
The bluebottle
Two-thousand
Year of the white bone:
Moscow:
The green fly.
Two-thousand,
The year of the hum:
New York:
The blue sleep
And the champion movie
Smiles at last
Too many creeps have won.

69

(VITAL IMPERATIVES FOR CHESTER)

1. Move that system.
2. Eat more chunks and get young.
3. Own a doll that glows.
4. Swallow cash.
5. Advance and have words with Barbecue.
6. Make noise in bed.
7. Treat yourself to the national experience.
8. Move while stopping and save Bucks.
9. Have bliss in presidential Suburb.
10. Form large bends in those rooms.
11. Have fun with secret radio beams.
12. Open advice space with fatigue piston.
13. Mesh with liberal motives at model home.
14. Desire dermal gloves.
15. Imitate loss of heat needs and sprint.
16. Go drink China Sea.
17. Be a beautiful soul with St. Joseph.

18. Let lucky numbers change your mind.
19. Invite President to defy reality: he fights for YOU.
20. Get with new worlds in nearest Church.
21. Now imitate empty space.
22. Dig good will fronts and phase out.
23. Mulch it.
24. Ape that red trace.
25. Invent giant molars.
26. After the demonstration: bring Catchmouse* to the autopsy.

70

DRAMAS OF THE EVENING

Clean-cut pirate meets and befriends priceless stolen owl.
Hidden monument is found living in pleasure-dome with friend.
Owl and stolen friend co-star in Oliver Twist as portrayed by select flames.

Beautiful clever custard woman wills free costume in silent chairs.
Posing space-man compares expert with captive church-leaders.
Rose woman disguised as science-chief is mistaken for stolen owl.
Expert hero leaving uptown college becomes survivor of Trojan war.
Secret outlaw laboratory on burning ranch is scene of activities:
Owl is shown transforming space-scientists into animals.

* Catchmouse = a famous cat.

Rocket woman teaches available outlaws to operate
   health club in frozen surroundings.
Owl seeks friend who betrayed safety zone with winning
   wrecks.
Keepers, inducing animals to contact invisible author,
   expand trial phones.

Subliminal engineer meets Little Red Riding Hood in
chains and learns love-secrets of best looking fugitives
thru' Thursday.

Artistic duck unmasks owl in underground French
scene: they trace exotic animal forces to latent technique.
Dream interpretation explained as new Funny Girl
comes home with banner exceptions in blindfold plot.
She turns gypsy in visual premises beyond any known
shore. Job's queen reclines forever on a beautiful board.

Sham doctor arrives in flying saucer welcomed by nor-
mal-type kids and gives pain. Wonderful contrived
movement of astrobabes in coptic reservation compound.
Animated clergy storms conceptual void in theo-drama
while Deity groans. Owls and health-buffs take over
haunted network.

Buffs destroy owls with sardonic asides and expert de-
plores incandescence of young ferns.

Riot woman transformed into savings bonds is traced to
unforgettable swans for the entire ruin of one season.

71

Adventure of Giomar: Castilian football
Minding doctrines

All night. Fire Harbor
The sky
A cataract. Unforeseen
Borealis
There is nothing left
Send supplies, medicine
And more wine
Cordially.

72

Morning. Good for foliage to resist the faithful wind.
Lean into new light. Listen to well-ordered hills go by,
rank upon rank, in the sun. The heat will soon blaze
blue and white. The long frying of September in the
shallow pan of fields. The sound of the earth goes up to
embrace the constant sky. My own center is the teeming
heart of natural families.

73

Determined to love
Lured by the barbarous fowl
He enters the rusty thicket of wires
Where nothing is tame

He meets his artiste
Who invites him to her ballet
There the swimming head
Makes everybody bleed.

Hanging on the wires
Love is still warm
A breakfast bird:
Eat your winged food!

Eat and go crazy
So crazy you have to fly
It is more than you will ever need!

Dizzy with spectacles
He admires her folly
Her breakfast dance.

He studies each new day's
Article of faith
The engaging records
Of broken heights

The moon is the delight
Of carnival waters
The sun is booming
In cannibal joy

By degrees their liturgy
Becomes rapacious
By degrees
Their careless boat goes down

Determined to love
In the sharp-eyed ocean
He follows all pirates
To the whirlpools.

74

O God do I have to be Wordsworth
Striding on the Blue Fells
With a lake for sale and Lucy
Locked in the hole of my camera?

Why do I ruin my whole life
Proclaiming the sorrows of animals
Which I keep in a pack on my shoulder?
Once when I met the Vegetable King
On the way to market
He said something that set me thinking.

"Coleridge," he said, "you bloody fool
Why do you stride over the Blue Fells
Swimming in Walden Pond
In that old football uniform:
Buy yourself an automobile!"

Yet in my heart I knew he had me
Figured for a minister: which is wrong
I am sustained
By ravens only and by the fancies
Of female benefactors.

Better to study the germinating waters of my wood
And know this fever: or die in a distant country
Having become a pure cone
Or turn to my eastern abstinence
With that old inscrutable love cry
And describe a perfect circle.

75

I seek you in the hospital where you work. Will you be
a patch of white moving rapidly across the end of the
next hall? I begin again in every shadow, surrounded by
the sound of scandal and the buzzer calling all doctors
to the presence of alarm.

76

After that we'll meet in some Kingdom they forgot and there the found will play the songs of the sent. Surely a big bird with all the shades of light will beat against our windows. We will then gladly consent to the kindness of rays and recover the warm knowledge of each other we once had under those young trees in another May. (It is a big bird flies right out of the center of the sun.)

77

Angels again
Farmers of the mind
In its flowers and fevers
Fishers in the blue revolutions of oil

They find me always upside down
In these reflected glooms
Lost in the wide rain's
Foundering accelerations

They walk with me
Through the shivering scrap-towns
And clearly show me how to cross
The dubious and elastic
Rail way
To weight weightless
Manuscript burdens

As I become fast freight
A perishing express
To the countries of the dead
In salt water flights
And unprotested weeping
Of old churches

I am an entire sensate parcel
Of registered earth
Working my way through adolescence
To swim dashing storms
Of amusement and attend
The copyrighted tornado
Of sheer sound

Though metal strings
Complain of my mind's eye
Nine fond harmonies
Never leave me alone

Till towns are built bone dry
With vigils and stones
Plate glass music
And oracular houses
Of earth spent calm
Long comas of the propitious time

O heavenly departures
With all the numbered bones
And the perfumes.

78

(THE HARMONIES OF EXCESS)

The hidden lovers in the soil
Become green plants and gardens tomorrow
When they are ordered to re-appear
In the wet sun's poem

Then they force the delighted
Power of buds to laugh louder
They scatter all the cries of light

Like shadow rain and make their bed
Over and over in the hollow flower
The violet bonfire

They spin the senses of the mute morning
In an abandoned river
Love's wreckage is then left to lie
All around the breathless shores
Of my voice
Which on the coasts of larking meadows
Invented all these children and their mischievous noises

So those lovers teach April stars
To riot rebel and follow faithless courses
And it doesn't matter
The seed is not afraid
Of winter or the terrible sweetness
Of the spring's convivial nightmare
Or the hot surprise and dizzy spark
Of their electric promise

For the lovers in the sleeping nerve
Are the hope and the address
Where I send you this burning garden
My talkative morning-glory
My climbing germ of poems.

79

O it is not lazy to be a messenger or to live out of the
shadow of some town. Other masks would be less
trouble. This one is never allowed to be familiar: it is
often the most naked. It is not without risk in a season
of frost. Nothing that is chosen is unbearable.

80

Slowly slowly
Comes Christ through the garden
Speaking to the sacred trees
Their branches bear his light
Without harm

Slowly slowly
Comes Christ through the ruins
Seeking the lost disciple
A timid one
Too literate
To believe words
So he hides

Slowly slowly
Christ rises on the cornfields
It is only the harvest moon
The disciple
Turns over in his sleep
And murmurs:
"My regret!"

The disciple will awaken
When he knows history
But slowly slowly
The Lord of History
Weeps into the fire.

81

Not to be without words in a season of effort. Not to be
without a vow in the summer of harvest. What have the

signs promised on the lonely hill? Word and work have their measure, and so does pain. Look in your own life and see if you find it.

82

It rained dark and cold on the Day of St. Theresa of the
  Heart
For no one yet knew that it was holiday fifteen
It rained like weather in honor of her sacred love
For the notables had built a black stone wall around her
  heart
And the prelates, mayors, and confessors wanted the
  doors closed.
The tongue of her heart, they said, must proffer insults
  to the vision.
So they built four walls of cold rain around the vision.
And the rain came down upon the vision in honor of
  her love.
In the theological cell where she was locked alone with
  the vision
Her heart was pierced by a thousand needles of fire.
Then the mayors, prelates, and confessors all wept to-
  gether in honor of her love.
They went together in procession to the rainy city walls
  and fortified
Their minds, wrapping them in the folds of the black
  storm.
Behind them in the invisible town the jails and convents
  overflowed with flame.
In the smallest window of all St. Theresa
Forgotten by these entranced jokers turned her heart
  into a dove.
The rain ended at that moment.
The dove had flown into the fiery center of the vision.

83

(SOLEMN MUSIC)

Use your numbered line
To describe constellations
Hunter and Capricorn
And heavenly Bears
Amid *Sanctus* sounds
And transports
The golden fury of wires

The lighted years
Of distant space
Are all made human
By modes of music
The questioning *vox humana*
The disciplines of chant

Take your compasses
To measure flight
Expanding silences
And pay attention
To the stillness of the end
Or the beginning
Sanctus
The abyss of brass
The sapphire orchestra

Bear the hot
Well-fired shot
Roaring out
Of the cool dark

And go to meet
In the wet estranged country

The midnight express
Bringing Plato, Prophets, Milton, Blake,
The nine daughters of memory

But use your own numbered line
To go down alone
Into the night sky
Hand over hand
And dig it like a mine.

84

Gelassenheit:
Desert and void. The Uncreated is waste and emptiness
to the creature. Not even sand. Not even stone. Not even
darkness and night. A burning wilderness would at
least be "something." It burns and is wild. But the
Uncreated is no something. Waste. Emptiness. Total
poverty of the Creator: yet from this poverty springs
everything. The waste is inexhaustible. Infinite Zero.
Everything comes from this desert Nothing. Everything
wants to return to it and cannot. For who can return
"nowhere?" But for each of us there is a point of no-
whereness in the middle of movement, a point of nothingness in the midst of being: the incomparable point,
not to be discovered by insight. If you seek it you do not
find it. If you stop seeking, it is there. But you must
not turn to it. Once you become aware of yourself as
seeker, you are lost. But if you are content to be lost you
will be found without knowing it, precisely because
you are lost, for you are, at last, nowhere.

85

The flash of falling metals. The shower of parts,
cameras, guns of experience in the waste heaven of
deadly rays. Cataclysm of designs. Out of the meteor sky

cascades the efficient rage of our team. Down comes another blazing and dissolute unit melting in mid-air over a fortunate suburb. A perishing computer blazes down into a figure of fire and steam. We live under the rain of stainless leaders. They strike themselves out like matches and fizz for our conjecture in the streets of Taurus. Gone is another technical spy in giant and instant heat. Gone is another tested explorer. Gone is another brilliant intuition of an engineer.

86

"The true word of eternity is spoken only in the spirit of that man who is himself a wilderness." (Eckhart)
"It is only the shadow of God which enlightened our inward wilderness: but on the high mountains of the Promised Land there is no shadow." (Ruysbroeck)

87

I am about to make my home
In the bell's summit
Set my mind a thousand feet high
On the ace of songs
In a mood of needles and random lights
To purify
The quick magnetic sodas of the skin

I will call the deep protectors out of the ground
The givers of wine
The writers of peace and waste
And sundown riddles

The threat of winter gleams in gray-haired windows
And witty mirrors
And fear lies over the sea

DATE DUE

8-21			

GAYLORD   PRINTED IN U.S.A.